50 Beginner Casserole Creation Recipes for Home

By: Kelly Johnson

Table of Contents

- Classic Macaroni and Cheese Casserole
- Chicken and Rice Casserole
- Taco Casserole
- Vegetable Lasagna
- Cheesy Broccoli and Rice Casserole
- Beef and Noodle Casserole
- Baked Ziti
- Tuna Noodle Casserole
- Stuffed Bell Pepper Casserole
- Potato and Ham Casserole
- Chili Mac Casserole
- Egg and Sausage Breakfast Casserole
- Creamy Mushroom and Spinach Casserole
- BBQ Chicken Casserole
- Italian Sausage and Peppers Casserole
- Quinoa and Black Bean Casserole
- Creamy Chicken and Broccoli Casserole
- Sausage and Cheese Biscuit Casserole
- Sweet Potato and Black Bean Casserole
- Chicken Alfredo Pasta Bake
- Ratatouille Casserole
- Vegetarian Enchilada Casserole
- Cabbage Roll Casserole
- Buffalo Chicken Casserole
- Cornbread and Sausage Casserole
- Eggplant Parmesan Casserole
- Creamy Tomato and Basil Casserole
- Zucchini and Tomato Gratin
- Potato and Cheese Casserole
- French Toast Casserole
- Meatball Casserole
- Bacon and Egg Casserole
- Seafood Rice Casserole
- Vegetable and Cheese Casserole
- Sloppy Joe Casserole
- Crispy Chicken Casserole

- Pasta Primavera Casserole
- Spinach and Feta Casserole
- Shepherd's Pie Casserole
- Teriyaki Chicken Casserole
- Pork Chop and Rice Casserole
- Three Cheese Pasta Bake
- Savory Breakfast Casserole
- Mushroom and Cheese Quinoa Casserole
- Peanut Butter and Banana Overnight Casserole
- Cheesy Cauliflower Casserole
- Mediterranean Chickpea Casserole
- Loaded Baked Potato Casserole
- Turkey and Stuffing Casserole
- Apple Crisp Casserole

Classic Macaroni and Cheese Casserole

Ingredients:

- 8 oz elbow macaroni
- 2 cups sharp cheddar cheese, shredded
- 1 cup mozzarella cheese, shredded
- 3 cups milk
- 1/4 cup butter
- 1/4 cup all-purpose flour
- 1 tsp mustard powder
- 1/2 tsp garlic powder
- Salt and pepper to taste
- 1 cup breadcrumbs (optional, for topping)

Instructions:

1. Preheat your oven to 350°F (175°C).
2. Cook macaroni according to package instructions; drain and set aside.
3. In a saucepan, melt butter over medium heat. Whisk in flour, cooking for 1-2 minutes.
4. Gradually add milk, stirring until thickened. Add mustard powder, garlic powder, salt, and pepper.
5. Stir in 2 cups of cheddar and all mozzarella until melted.
6. Combine cheese sauce with macaroni and pour into a greased casserole dish. Top with remaining cheddar and breadcrumbs if using.
7. Bake for 25-30 minutes, until bubbly and golden.

Enjoy your ultimate comfort food!

Chicken and Rice Casserole

Ingredients:

- 2 cups cooked chicken, shredded
- 1 cup long-grain rice
- 2 cups chicken broth
- 1 can cream of mushroom soup
- 1 cup frozen mixed vegetables
- 1 tsp garlic powder
- Salt and pepper to taste
- 1 cup cheddar cheese, shredded
  Instructions:
1. Preheat oven to 350°F (175°C).
2. In a large bowl, mix all ingredients except cheese.
3. Pour into a greased casserole dish.
4. Cover with foil and bake for 45 minutes.
5. Remove foil, sprinkle cheese on top, and bake for an additional 15 minutes until cheese is melted.

Taco Casserole

Ingredients:

- 1 lb ground beef
- 1 packet taco seasoning
- 1 can black beans, drained
- 1 cup corn
- 2 cups tortilla chips
- 2 cups cheddar cheese, shredded
- 1 cup salsa
- Chopped green onions for garnish

Instructions:

1. Preheat oven to 350°F (175°C).
2. Brown the ground beef in a skillet and stir in taco seasoning.
3. In a greased casserole dish, layer chips, beef mixture, beans, corn, salsa, and cheese.
4. Bake for 20-25 minutes until heated through and cheese is bubbly.
5. Garnish with green onions.

Vegetable Lasagna

Ingredients:

- 9 lasagna noodles
- 2 cups ricotta cheese
- 2 cups spinach (fresh or frozen)
- 2 cups marinara sauce
- 2 cups mixed vegetables (zucchini, bell peppers, mushrooms)
- 2 cups mozzarella cheese, shredded
- 1/2 cup Parmesan cheese, grated
- Salt and pepper to taste

Instructions:

1. Preheat oven to 375°F (190°C).
2. Cook lasagna noodles according to package instructions; drain.
3. In a baking dish, spread a layer of marinara sauce, then a layer of noodles, followed by ricotta, spinach, mixed vegetables, and mozzarella. Repeat layers, finishing with noodles and remaining sauce.
4. Top with mozzarella and Parmesan.
5. Cover with foil and bake for 30 minutes, then uncover and bake for another 15 minutes until bubbly.

Cheesy Broccoli and Rice Casserole

Ingredients:

- 2 cups cooked rice
- 2 cups broccoli florets, steamed
- 1 can cream of chicken soup
- 1 cup milk
- 2 cups cheddar cheese, shredded
- 1/2 cup onion, diced
- Salt and pepper to taste
- 1 cup breadcrumbs (optional, for topping)

Instructions:

1. Preheat oven to 350°F (175°C).
2. In a large bowl, combine rice, broccoli, soup, milk, onion, salt, pepper, and 1 1/2 cups cheese.
3. Pour mixture into a greased casserole dish.
4. Top with remaining cheese and breadcrumbs if using.
5. Bake for 25-30 minutes until heated through and cheese is melted.

Enjoy these delicious casseroles!

Beef and Noodle Casserole

Ingredients:

- 1 lb ground beef
- 1 onion, diced
- 2 cups egg noodles, cooked
- 1 can cream of mushroom soup
- 1 cup beef broth
- 1 cup cheddar cheese, shredded
- Salt and pepper to taste
  Instructions:
1. Preheat oven to 350°F (175°C).
2. In a skillet, brown ground beef and onion; drain excess fat.
3. In a large bowl, combine cooked noodles, beef mixture, soup, broth, salt, and pepper.
4. Pour into a greased casserole dish and top with cheese.
5. Bake for 25-30 minutes until bubbly.

Baked Ziti

Ingredients:

- 1 lb ziti pasta
- 2 cups marinara sauce
- 1 cup ricotta cheese
- 2 cups mozzarella cheese, shredded
- 1/2 cup Parmesan cheese, grated
- 1 tsp Italian seasoning
- Salt and pepper to taste

Instructions:

1. Preheat oven to 375°F (190°C).
2. Cook ziti according to package instructions; drain.
3. In a bowl, mix cooked pasta, marinara sauce, ricotta, Italian seasoning, salt, and pepper.
4. Pour into a greased baking dish and top with mozzarella and Parmesan.
5. Bake for 25-30 minutes until cheese is melted and golden.

Tuna Noodle Casserole

Ingredients:

- 2 cans tuna, drained
- 2 cups egg noodles, cooked
- 1 can cream of celery soup
- 1 cup frozen peas
- 1 cup cheddar cheese, shredded
- 1/2 cup milk
- Salt and pepper to taste

Instructions:

1. Preheat oven to 350°F (175°C).
2. In a bowl, combine tuna, cooked noodles, soup, peas, milk, salt, and pepper.
3. Pour into a greased casserole dish and top with cheese.
4. Bake for 25-30 minutes until heated through.

Stuffed Bell Pepper Casserole

Ingredients:

- 4 bell peppers, chopped
- 1 lb ground beef
- 1 cup cooked rice
- 1 can diced tomatoes
- 1 cup mozzarella cheese, shredded
- 1 tsp Italian seasoning
- Salt and pepper to taste

Instructions:

1. Preheat oven to 375°F (190°C).
2. In a skillet, brown ground beef; drain excess fat.
3. In a bowl, mix beef, rice, chopped peppers, tomatoes, Italian seasoning, salt, and pepper.
4. Pour into a greased casserole dish and top with mozzarella.
5. Bake for 30-35 minutes until peppers are tender.

Potato and Ham Casserole

Ingredients:

- 4 cups diced potatoes
- 2 cups cooked ham, diced
- 1 can cream of mushroom soup
- 1 cup milk
- 2 cups cheddar cheese, shredded
- Salt and pepper to taste
  Instructions:
1. Preheat oven to 350°F (175°C).
2. In a large bowl, mix potatoes, ham, soup, milk, salt, and pepper.
3. Pour into a greased baking dish and top with cheese.
4. Bake for 45-50 minutes until potatoes are tender and cheese is bubbly.

Chili Mac Casserole

Ingredients:

- 1 lb ground beef
- 1 can chili (with or without beans)
- 2 cups elbow macaroni, cooked
- 1 cup shredded cheese (cheddar or Monterey Jack)
- 1/2 cup onion, diced
- Salt and pepper to taste

Instructions:

1. Preheat oven to 350°F (175°C).
2. In a skillet, brown ground beef and onion; drain excess fat.
3. In a bowl, combine beef mixture, chili, cooked macaroni, salt, and pepper.
4. Pour into a greased casserole dish and top with cheese.
5. Bake for 20-25 minutes until cheese is melted.

Egg and Sausage Breakfast Casserole

Ingredients:

- 1 lb breakfast sausage, cooked and crumbled
- 6 eggs
- 1 cup milk
- 2 cups hash browns
- 1 cup cheddar cheese, shredded
- Salt and pepper to taste
  Instructions:
1. Preheat oven to 350°F (175°C).
2. In a greased casserole dish, layer hash browns and cooked sausage.
3. In a bowl, whisk together eggs, milk, salt, and pepper; pour over sausage.
4. Top with cheese and bake for 30-35 minutes until eggs are set.

Creamy Mushroom and Spinach Casserole

Ingredients:

- 2 cups fresh spinach
- 1 cup mushrooms, sliced
- 1 cup cream of mushroom soup
- 1/2 cup sour cream
- 1 cup cooked rice
- 1 cup cheddar cheese, shredded
- Salt and pepper to taste

Instructions:
1. Preheat oven to 350°F (175°C).
2. In a skillet, sauté mushrooms until tender; add spinach and cook until wilted.
3. In a bowl, combine sautéed vegetables, soup, sour cream, rice, salt, and pepper.
4. Pour into a greased casserole dish and top with cheese.
5. Bake for 25-30 minutes until heated through and cheese is melted.

Enjoy these hearty casseroles!

BBQ Chicken Casserole

Ingredients:

- 2 cups cooked chicken, shredded
- 1 cup BBQ sauce
- 2 cups cooked rice
- 1 cup corn
- 1 cup cheddar cheese, shredded
- 1/2 cup green onions, sliced
   Instructions:
1. Preheat oven to 350°F (175°C).
2. In a bowl, mix chicken, BBQ sauce, rice, corn, and green onions.
3. Pour into a greased casserole dish and top with cheese.
4. Bake for 25-30 minutes until bubbly.

Italian Sausage and Peppers Casserole

Ingredients:

- 1 lb Italian sausage, sliced
- 2 bell peppers, sliced
- 1 onion, sliced
- 1 can diced tomatoes
- 2 cups penne pasta, cooked
- 1 cup mozzarella cheese, shredded

Instructions:

1. Preheat oven to 375°F (190°C).
2. In a skillet, brown sausage; add peppers and onion, cooking until tender.
3. In a bowl, mix sausage mixture, tomatoes, and cooked pasta.
4. Pour into a greased dish and top with mozzarella.
5. Bake for 20-25 minutes until cheese is melted.

Quinoa and Black Bean Casserole

Ingredients:

- 1 cup quinoa, rinsed
- 1 can black beans, drained
- 1 cup corn
- 1 can diced tomatoes
- 1 tsp cumin
- 1 cup cheddar cheese, shredded
  Instructions:
1. Preheat oven to 350°F (175°C).
2. In a bowl, combine quinoa, black beans, corn, tomatoes, cumin, salt, and pepper.
3. Pour into a greased casserole dish and top with cheese.
4. Bake for 30-35 minutes until quinoa is cooked.

Creamy Chicken and Broccoli Casserole

Ingredients:

- 2 cups cooked chicken, shredded
- 2 cups broccoli florets, steamed
- 1 can cream of chicken soup
- 1 cup milk
- 1 cup cheddar cheese, shredded
- 1 cup breadcrumbs (optional, for topping)

Instructions:

1. Preheat oven to 350°F (175°C).
2. In a bowl, mix chicken, broccoli, soup, milk, and cheese.
3. Pour into a greased dish and top with breadcrumbs if using.
4. Bake for 25-30 minutes until heated through and bubbly.

Sausage and Cheese Biscuit Casserole

Ingredients:

- 1 lb breakfast sausage, cooked and crumbled
- 1 can refrigerated biscuit dough, cut into pieces
- 6 eggs
- 1 cup milk
- 1 cup cheddar cheese, shredded
- Salt and pepper to taste
  Instructions:
1. Preheat oven to 350°F (175°C).
2. In a greased casserole dish, layer biscuit pieces and cooked sausage.
3. In a bowl, whisk together eggs, milk, salt, and pepper; pour over sausage.
4. Top with cheese and bake for 30-35 minutes until eggs are set.

Sweet Potato and Black Bean Casserole

Ingredients:

- 2 cups sweet potatoes, peeled and diced
- 1 can black beans, drained
- 1 cup corn
- 1 tsp chili powder
- 1 cup shredded cheese (cheddar or Monterey Jack)

Instructions:

1. Preheat oven to 375°F (190°C).
2. In a bowl, combine sweet potatoes, black beans, corn, chili powder, salt, and pepper.
3. Pour into a greased dish and top with cheese.
4. Bake for 30-35 minutes until sweet potatoes are tender.

Chicken Alfredo Pasta Bake

Ingredients:

- 2 cups cooked pasta (penne or rotini)
- 2 cups cooked chicken, shredded
- 2 cups Alfredo sauce
- 1 cup broccoli florets, steamed
- 1 cup mozzarella cheese, shredded

Instructions:

1. Preheat oven to 350°F (175°C).
2. In a bowl, mix pasta, chicken, Alfredo sauce, and broccoli.
3. Pour into a greased casserole dish and top with mozzarella.
4. Bake for 25-30 minutes until heated through and cheese is melted.

Enjoy these flavorful casseroles!

Ratatouille Casserole

Ingredients:

- 1 eggplant, diced
- 2 zucchini, sliced
- 1 bell pepper, diced
- 1 onion, chopped
- 2 cups diced tomatoes (canned or fresh)
- 2 cloves garlic, minced
- 1 tsp dried thyme
- 1 tsp dried basil
- Salt and pepper to taste
- 1 cup mozzarella cheese, shredded

Instructions:

1. Preheat oven to 375°F (190°C).
2. In a large skillet, sauté onion and garlic until softened.
3. Add eggplant, zucchini, and bell pepper; cook until tender.
4. Stir in tomatoes, thyme, basil, salt, and pepper; cook for 5 minutes.
5. Pour mixture into a greased casserole dish, top with mozzarella, and bake for 25-30 minutes until bubbly.

Vegetarian Enchilada Casserole

Ingredients:

- 6 corn tortillas, cut into strips
- 1 can black beans, drained
- 1 can corn, drained
- 1 cup diced bell peppers
- 2 cups enchilada sauce
- 1 cup cheddar cheese, shredded
- 1 tsp cumin
- 1 tsp chili powder

Instructions:

1. Preheat oven to 350°F (175°C).
2. In a bowl, mix black beans, corn, bell peppers, cumin, and chili powder.
3. In a greased casserole dish, layer tortillas, bean mixture, enchilada sauce, and cheese.
4. Repeat layers, finishing with cheese on top.
5. Bake for 25-30 minutes until heated through and cheese is melted.

Cabbage Roll Casserole

Ingredients:

- 1 lb ground beef or turkey
- 1 onion, diced
- 4 cups chopped cabbage
- 2 cups cooked rice
- 1 can diced tomatoes
- 1 cup tomato sauce
- 1 tsp Italian seasoning
- Salt and pepper to taste

Instructions:

1. Preheat oven to 350°F (175°C).
2. In a skillet, brown the meat with onion; drain excess fat.
3. In a bowl, combine cooked meat, cabbage, rice, tomatoes, tomato sauce, Italian seasoning, salt, and pepper.
4. Pour mixture into a greased casserole dish and bake for 45 minutes until cabbage is tender.

Buffalo Chicken Casserole

Ingredients:

- 2 cups cooked chicken, shredded
- 1 cup buffalo sauce
- 2 cups cooked pasta (rotini or penne)
- 1 cup ranch dressing
- 1 cup cheddar cheese, shredded
  Instructions:
1. Preheat oven to 350°F (175°C).
2. In a bowl, mix chicken, buffalo sauce, pasta, and ranch dressing.
3. Pour into a greased casserole dish and top with cheese.
4. Bake for 20-25 minutes until heated through and cheese is melted.

Cornbread and Sausage Casserole

Ingredients:

- 1 lb breakfast sausage, cooked and crumbled
- 1 box cornbread mix, prepared
- 1 cup cheddar cheese, shredded
- 4 eggs
- 1 cup milk
- Salt and pepper to taste

Instructions:

1. Preheat oven to 375°F (190°C).
2. In a bowl, mix cornbread mix, eggs, milk, salt, and pepper.
3. Stir in cooked sausage and cheese.
4. Pour into a greased baking dish and bake for 25-30 minutes until golden and set.

Eggplant Parmesan Casserole

Ingredients:

- 2 eggplants, sliced
- 2 cups marinara sauce
- 1 cup ricotta cheese
- 1 cup mozzarella cheese, shredded
- 1/2 cup Parmesan cheese, grated
- 1 tsp Italian seasoning

Instructions:

1. Preheat oven to 375°F (190°C).
2. In a greased casserole dish, layer eggplant, marinara sauce, ricotta, mozzarella, and Italian seasoning.
3. Repeat layers, finishing with mozzarella and Parmesan on top.
4. Bake for 30-35 minutes until bubbly and golden.

Creamy Tomato and Basil Casserole

Ingredients:

- 2 cups cooked pasta (penne or rotini)
- 2 cups cherry tomatoes, halved
- 1 cup heavy cream
- 1 cup fresh basil, chopped
- 1 cup mozzarella cheese, shredded
- Salt and pepper to taste

Instructions:

1. Preheat oven to 350°F (175°C).
2. In a bowl, combine pasta, tomatoes, cream, basil, salt, and pepper.
3. Pour into a greased casserole dish and top with mozzarella.
4. Bake for 25-30 minutes until heated through and cheese is melted.

Zucchini and Tomato Gratin

Ingredients:

- 3 zucchinis, sliced
- 3 tomatoes, sliced
- 1 onion, sliced
- 1 cup breadcrumbs
- 1 cup Parmesan cheese, grated
- 2 tbsp olive oil
- Salt and pepper to taste
  Instructions:
1. Preheat oven to 375°F (190°C).
2. In a greased casserole dish, layer zucchini, tomatoes, and onion.
3. Drizzle with olive oil, and sprinkle with salt, pepper, breadcrumbs, and Parmesan.
4. Bake for 30-35 minutes until golden and vegetables are tender.

Enjoy these delicious and hearty casseroles!

Potato and Cheese Casserole

Ingredients:

- 4 cups diced potatoes
- 1 cup sour cream
- 1 cup cheddar cheese, shredded
- 1/2 cup onion, diced
- 1 can cream of chicken soup
- Salt and pepper to taste

Instructions:

1. Preheat oven to 350°F (175°C).
2. In a large bowl, combine potatoes, sour cream, cheese, onion, soup, salt, and pepper.
3. Pour into a greased casserole dish and bake for 45-50 minutes until potatoes are tender.

French Toast Casserole

Ingredients:

- 8 slices bread, cubed
- 6 eggs
- 2 cups milk
- 1/2 cup maple syrup
- 1 tsp vanilla extract
- 1 tsp cinnamon

Instructions:

1. Preheat oven to 350°F (175°C).
2. In a greased casserole dish, layer cubed bread.
3. In a bowl, whisk together eggs, milk, syrup, vanilla, and cinnamon; pour over bread.
4. Bake for 30-35 minutes until set and golden.

Meatball Casserole

Ingredients:

- 1 lb frozen meatballs
- 2 cups marinara sauce
- 2 cups cooked pasta (penne or rotini)
- 1 cup mozzarella cheese, shredded
- 1/2 cup Parmesan cheese, grated

Instructions:

1. Preheat oven to 350°F (175°C).
2. In a bowl, combine meatballs, marinara, and cooked pasta.
3. Pour into a greased casserole dish and top with mozzarella and Parmesan.
4. Bake for 25-30 minutes until heated through and cheese is bubbly.

Bacon and Egg Casserole

Ingredients:

- 8 slices bacon, cooked and crumbled
- 6 eggs
- 1 cup milk
- 2 cups bread, cubed
- 1 cup cheddar cheese, shredded
- Salt and pepper to taste

Instructions:

1. Preheat oven to 350°F (175°C).
2. In a bowl, whisk together eggs, milk, salt, and pepper.
3. In a greased casserole dish, layer bread, bacon, and cheese.
4. Pour egg mixture over the top and bake for 30-35 minutes until set.

Seafood Rice Casserole

Ingredients:

- 2 cups cooked rice
- 1 lb seafood mix (shrimp, crab, etc.)
- 1 can cream of mushroom soup
- 1 cup milk
- 1 cup cheddar cheese, shredded
- 1/2 cup green onions, sliced

Instructions:

1. Preheat oven to 350°F (175°C).
2. In a bowl, combine rice, seafood, soup, milk, cheese, and green onions.
3. Pour into a greased casserole dish and bake for 25-30 minutes until heated through.

Vegetable and Cheese Casserole

Ingredients:

- 2 cups mixed vegetables (carrots, peas, corn)
- 1 cup cheddar cheese, shredded
- 1 cup cream of mushroom soup
- 1/2 cup milk
- 1 cup breadcrumbs (optional, for topping)
  Instructions:
1. Preheat oven to 350°F (175°C).
2. In a bowl, mix vegetables, cheese, soup, and milk.
3. Pour into a greased casserole dish and top with breadcrumbs if using.
4. Bake for 25-30 minutes until bubbly.

Sloppy Joe Casserole

Ingredients:

- 1 lb ground beef
- 1 cup Sloppy Joe sauce
- 2 cups cooked pasta (elbow macaroni)
- 1 cup cheddar cheese, shredded
- 1/2 cup onion, diced

Instructions:

1. Preheat oven to 350°F (175°C).
2. In a skillet, brown ground beef and onion; drain excess fat.
3. Stir in Sloppy Joe sauce and cooked pasta.
4. Pour into a greased casserole dish and top with cheese.
5. Bake for 20-25 minutes until heated through and cheese is melted.

Crispy Chicken Casserole

Ingredients:

- 2 cups cooked chicken, shredded
- 1 cup cream of chicken soup
- 1 cup sour cream
- 2 cups cooked rice
- 1 cup crushed cornflakes (for topping)
- Salt and pepper to taste
   Instructions:
1. Preheat oven to 350°F (175°C).
2. In a bowl, mix chicken, soup, sour cream, rice, salt, and pepper.
3. Pour into a greased casserole dish and top with cornflakes.
4. Bake for 25-30 minutes until heated through and crispy on top.

Enjoy these comforting casseroles!

Pasta Primavera Casserole

Ingredients:

- 3 cups cooked pasta (penne or fusilli)
- 2 cups mixed vegetables (bell peppers, zucchini, carrots)
- 1 cup marinara sauce
- 1 cup mozzarella cheese, shredded
- 1/2 cup Parmesan cheese, grated
- 1 tsp Italian seasoning

Instructions:

1. Preheat oven to 375°F (190°C).
2. In a bowl, combine cooked pasta, vegetables, marinara, and Italian seasoning.
3. Pour into a greased casserole dish and top with mozzarella and Parmesan.
4. Bake for 25-30 minutes until heated through and cheese is bubbly.

Spinach and Feta Casserole

Ingredients:

- 2 cups fresh spinach, chopped
- 1 cup feta cheese, crumbled
- 6 eggs
- 1 cup milk
- 1 cup cooked rice
- Salt and pepper to taste

Instructions:

1. Preheat oven to 350°F (175°C).
2. In a greased casserole dish, layer spinach, feta, and cooked rice.
3. In a bowl, whisk together eggs, milk, salt, and pepper; pour over the top.
4. Bake for 30-35 minutes until set and golden.

Shepherd's Pie Casserole

Ingredients:

- 1 lb ground beef or lamb
- 1 cup frozen mixed vegetables
- 1 onion, diced
- 2 cups mashed potatoes
- 1 cup beef broth
- Salt and pepper to taste

Instructions:

1. Preheat oven to 350°F (175°C).
2. In a skillet, brown meat and onion; drain excess fat.
3. Stir in mixed vegetables, beef broth, salt, and pepper; simmer for 5 minutes.
4. Pour meat mixture into a greased dish, top with mashed potatoes, and bake for 25-30 minutes until heated through.

Teriyaki Chicken Casserole

Ingredients:

- 2 cups cooked chicken, shredded
- 1 cup teriyaki sauce
- 2 cups cooked rice
- 1 cup mixed vegetables (broccoli, carrots, snap peas)
- 1/2 cup green onions, sliced
  Instructions:
1. Preheat oven to 350°F (175°C).
2. In a bowl, mix chicken, teriyaki sauce, rice, and vegetables.
3. Pour into a greased casserole dish and sprinkle with green onions.
4. Bake for 25-30 minutes until heated through.

Pork Chop and Rice Casserole

Ingredients:

- 4 pork chops
- 1 cup uncooked rice
- 2 cups chicken broth
- 1 can cream of mushroom soup
- 1/2 cup onion, diced
- Salt and pepper to taste

Instructions:

1. Preheat oven to 350°F (175°C).
2. In a bowl, mix rice, broth, soup, onion, salt, and pepper.
3. Pour rice mixture into a greased casserole dish and place pork chops on top.
4. Bake for 45-50 minutes until pork is cooked through.

Three Cheese Pasta Bake

Ingredients:

- 2 cups cooked pasta (rigatoni or penne)
- 1 cup ricotta cheese
- 1 cup mozzarella cheese, shredded
- 1 cup Parmesan cheese, grated
- 2 cups marinara sauce
- 1 tsp Italian seasoning

Instructions:

1. Preheat oven to 375°F (190°C).
2. In a bowl, mix cooked pasta, ricotta, marinara, and Italian seasoning.
3. Pour into a greased dish and top with mozzarella and Parmesan.
4. Bake for 25-30 minutes until heated through and cheese is bubbly.

Savory Breakfast Casserole

Ingredients:

- 6 eggs
- 1 cup milk
- 1 lb breakfast sausage, cooked and crumbled
- 2 cups hash browns
- 1 cup cheddar cheese, shredded
- Salt and pepper to taste

Instructions:

1. Preheat oven to 350°F (175°C).
2. In a bowl, whisk together eggs, milk, salt, and pepper.
3. In a greased casserole dish, layer hash browns, sausage, and cheese.
4. Pour egg mixture over the top and bake for 30-35 minutes until set.

Mushroom and Cheese Quinoa Casserole

Ingredients:

- 2 cups cooked quinoa
- 2 cups mushrooms, sliced
- 1 cup spinach, chopped
- 1 cup cream of mushroom soup
- 1 cup mozzarella cheese, shredded
- Salt and pepper to taste

Instructions:

1. Preheat oven to 350°F (175°C).
2. In a skillet, sauté mushrooms until tender; add spinach and cook until wilted.
3. In a bowl, combine cooked quinoa, mushrooms, soup, salt, and pepper.
4. Pour into a greased casserole dish and top with cheese.
5. Bake for 25-30 minutes until heated through and cheese is melted.

Enjoy these delightful casseroles!

Peanut Butter and Banana Overnight Casserole

Ingredients:

- 2 cups old-fashioned oats
- 2 ripe bananas, sliced
- 1 cup milk (dairy or non-dairy)
- 1/2 cup peanut butter
- 1/4 cup maple syrup
- 1 tsp vanilla extract
- 1 tsp cinnamon
- 1/2 cup chopped nuts (optional)

Instructions:

1. In a large bowl, mix oats, bananas, milk, peanut butter, maple syrup, vanilla, and cinnamon.
2. Pour into a greased casserole dish, top with nuts if using.
3. Cover and refrigerate overnight.
4. In the morning, bake at 350°F (175°C) for 25-30 minutes until set.

Cheesy Cauliflower Casserole

Ingredients:

- 4 cups cauliflower florets
- 1 cup cheddar cheese, shredded
- 1/2 cup cream cheese
- 1/2 cup sour cream
- 1/4 cup grated Parmesan cheese
- 1/2 tsp garlic powder
- Salt and pepper to taste
  Instructions:
1. Preheat oven to 350°F (175°C).
2. Steam cauliflower until tender.
3. In a bowl, mix cheddar, cream cheese, sour cream, Parmesan, garlic powder, salt, and pepper.
4. Stir in cauliflower and pour into a greased casserole dish.
5. Bake for 25-30 minutes until bubbly and golden.

Mediterranean Chickpea Casserole

Ingredients:

- 2 cans chickpeas, drained and rinsed
- 1 cup cherry tomatoes, halved
- 1 bell pepper, diced
- 1/2 cup red onion, diced
- 1/2 cup feta cheese, crumbled
- 1/4 cup olive oil
- 2 tsp dried oregano
- Salt and pepper to taste
  Instructions:
1. Preheat oven to 375°F (190°C).
2. In a large bowl, combine chickpeas, tomatoes, bell pepper, onion, feta, olive oil, oregano, salt, and pepper.
3. Pour into a greased casserole dish and bake for 30-35 minutes until heated through.

Loaded Baked Potato Casserole

Ingredients:

- 4 large potatoes, baked and cubed
- 1 cup sour cream
- 1 cup cheddar cheese, shredded
- 1/2 cup cooked bacon, crumbled
- 1/4 cup green onions, sliced
- Salt and pepper to taste

Instructions:

1. Preheat oven to 350°F (175°C).
2. In a large bowl, mix potatoes, sour cream, cheese, bacon, green onions, salt, and pepper.
3. Pour into a greased casserole dish and bake for 25-30 minutes until heated through.

Turkey and Stuffing Casserole

Ingredients:

- 3 cups cooked turkey, shredded
- 1 can cream of chicken soup
- 1/2 cup milk
- 1 cup frozen mixed vegetables
- 1 box stuffing mix
- 1 cup chicken broth

Instructions:

1. Preheat oven to 350°F (175°C).
2. In a bowl, mix turkey, soup, milk, and vegetables.
3. Spread turkey mixture in a greased casserole dish.
4. In another bowl, combine stuffing mix and chicken broth; spoon over turkey.
5. Bake for 30-35 minutes until heated through and golden.

Apple Crisp Casserole

Ingredients:

- 4 cups sliced apples
- 1 cup brown sugar
- 1 cup oats
- 1/2 cup flour
- 1 tsp cinnamon
- 1/2 cup butter, melted

Instructions:

1. Preheat oven to 350°F (175°C).
2. In a greased casserole dish, layer sliced apples and sprinkle with cinnamon.
3. In a bowl, mix brown sugar, oats, flour, and melted butter until crumbly; sprinkle over apples.
4. Bake for 30-35 minutes until apples are tender and topping is golden.

Enjoy these delicious casseroles!

www.ingramcontent.com/pod-product-compliance
Lightning Source LLC
LaVergne TN
LVHW081331060526
838201LV00055B/2576